BEGINNING BLUES

Everything you need to know to become an accomplished perform

Text photographs by Caufield and Shook,
Courtesy of the University of Louisville, KY. (page 34)
Herbert Wise (pages 32, 36, 39, 42, 54),
Yazoo Records (pages 16, 29).

Order No. AM 35197
US International Standard Book Number: 0.8256.2353.7
UK International Standard Book Number: 0.7119.0453.7

Exclusive Distributors:
Music Sales Corporation
257 Park Avenue South, New York, NY 10010 USA
Music Sales Limited
8/9 Frith Street, London W1V 5TZ England
Music Sales Pty. Limited
120 Rothschild Street, Rosebery, Sydney, NSW 2018, Australia

Printed in the United States of America by
Vicks Lithograph and Printing Corporation

Amsco Publications
New York/London/Sydney

Contents

To the Student

When I first started piano lessons, I studied the classical masters—Mozart, Bach (my favorite), Beethoven, Schubert, Chopin, and others. I always had trouble reading through the pieces without adding (or subtracting) a few chords, or improvising around the melody. One of my teachers would scream "No, No, No!" at the piano's soundboard whenever I strayed from the printed music, and this would invariably agitate the neighbor's dogs. I soon realized that I didn't want to be a classical pianist.

So my fancy turned to jazz and blues. Unfortunately, there wasn't much music, or many books to learn from. I played Gershwin, tried pop tunes, Bartok and ragtime, and I turned to records for inspiration.

I'd spend hours and hours copying what I heard on records, tediously playing one phrase hundreds of times. It was learning by trial and error—mostly error.

My primary reason for writing *How To Play Blues Piano* is to give you the advantage of having blues music and instruction at your fingertips.

If you enjoy this book, make sure to continue by getting the other books and records mentioned in the back. Keep an open mind, make practicing a joyous experience, listen to everything, and the satisfaction you get will sustain you through the hard times.

To the Teacher

Teaching blues piano is a challenge. On one hand, the student must have the discipline to learn the basics; on the other, he must have the freedom to stray from the basics (or written music) when he is ready. It's my view that the teacher's job is to maintain the right balance, alternately pushing and restraining the student, and helping him discover his own inner expression.

How To Play Blues Piano presents the major styles and techniques essential for mastering the blues. Each chapter surveys a different style, from boogie woogie to barrelhouse, and introduces concepts like chord structure, blues tonality, bass lines, slides, and syncopation.

While all the pieces are simple, they are by no means simple-minded. I have made a determined effort to provide beginning material that retains the feeling and characteristics of more complex piano blues. The music increases in difficulty with each lesson, and provides a strong foundation for more advanced studies in blues and jazz piano styles.

The Basic Blues

All piano blues have a definite, predictable structure that musicians call a *blues progression.* In its most basic form, the blues progression is a combination of only three chords. For example, in the key of C major, the chords would be:

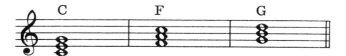

In the key of B♭ major, the blues progression chords are:

These three chords have many names in the language of music theory, but the easiest way to find them is to remember the numbers **1**, **6** and **8**. If you count up chromatically (white and black keys) on the keyboard, starting with any note (call it **1**), you'll find the other two chords of the blues progression at numbers **6** and **8**.

For example, suppose you choose D as **1**. Count up six keys (both black and white ones) and you'll find G. Count up eight keys from D and you'll find A. Thus D, G and A are the chords of a blues progression in the key of D.

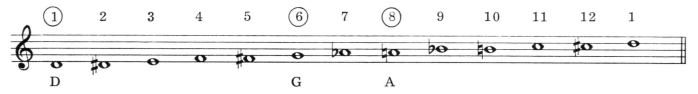

The basic blues progression is twelve measures long. In the key of C major, the pattern looks like this:

Musicians also use an eight-bar blues progression with the same general order of chords. This is the eight-bar blues in C major:

Practice these blues progressions until you've memorized the chord pattern. Then learn the pattern in the keys of F, G, B and D. Remember, use the 1-6-8 rule to find the right chords.

To help you memorize them, write out the twelve-bar blues for F, G, B and D on the staffs below:

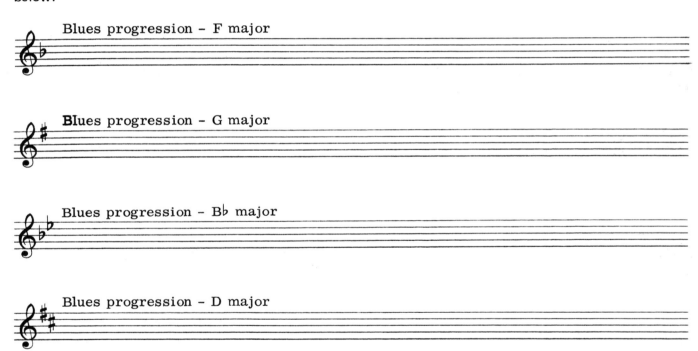

Because these three chords fall on the first, fourth and fifth notes of the major scale, this series is often called a I—IV—V progression.

Heartland Blues is a slow, twelve-bar blues in the key of F major. Practice slowly at first, until you have mastered the notes. Listen carefully to the moving notes in the left hand and notice how they "color" the entire piece.

Heartland Blues

Eric Kriss

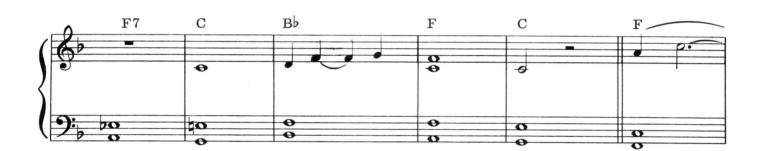

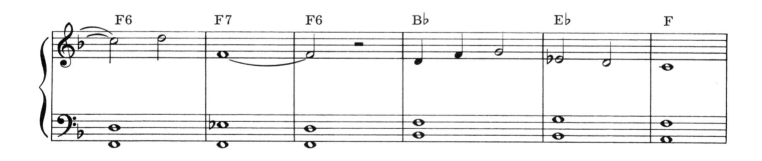

Blues Notes

Not all blues use the traditional blues progression described in the previous chapter, **The Basic Blues.** *House Of The Rising Sun*, for instance, is a very popular blues standard with a sixteen-bar progression quite different from most blues. *House of The Rising Sun* is classified as a blues not because of its progression, but because of its *tonality.* Tonality is the "color" that a piece of music captures through the use of chords and melody notes.

The concept of blues tonality is difficult to define with words. It is a musical feeling suggested by certain blues notes. Take the scale of C major, for example:

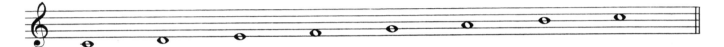

The two most important notes for getting a real bluesy feel are located near the third and seventh notes of the scale.

I say *near*, because these blues notes do not have an exact place in the scale of C major (or any other scale played on the piano). In a sense, they're "in-between" the keys. One is located about half way between B♭ and B natural, the other is between E♭ and E natural.

How can we play these "in-between" notes on the piano? Bluesmen have devised several special techniques, some of which will be described later, but one way of getting a blues tonality is to cleverly use the "approximate" blues notes in a song.

The arrangement of *House Of The Rising Sun* illustrates this clearly. You'll hear many different blues notes; some give the piece a major sound, others suggest a minor sound. This *ambiguity* is one secret of blues tonality because it helps create the impression of the "real" in-between blues notes.

House Of The Rising Sun is in 3/4 time—be sure to emphasize the first beat in each measure. Play the piece slowly with an even flow, and try to make the transitions from blues note to blues note as smoothly as possible.

House Of The Rising Sun

Traditional
Arranged by Eric Kriss

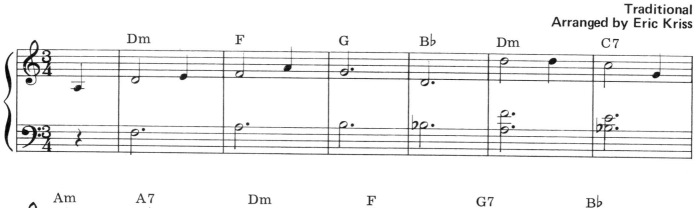

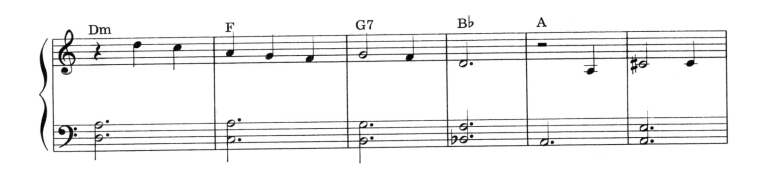

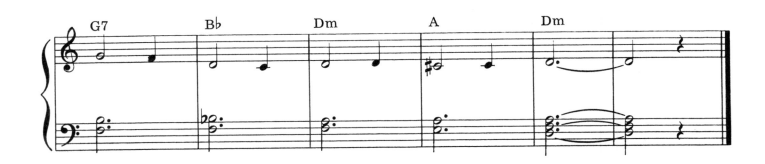

Folk Blues

Blues musicians use many sources of inspiration for their songs. Some are about particular events—Charley Patton relates the story of a Mississippi flood in *High Water Everywhere,* recorded in 1929. Some blues focus on geographical locations, like *Texas Blues* or Little Brother Montgomery's *Vicksburg Blues* (Vicksburg is a town in Mississippi), while other songs refer to politics, hard times or personal troubles—*Army Bound Blues, Poor Boy Blues,* and *Downhearted Mama* are a few samples.

Another kind of blues—folk blues—were adapted from older folk songs and don't have any known composer or place of origin. One famous tune, *See See Rider,* has been recorded thousands of times in every conceivable style. Well-known bluesmen, like Big Bill Broonzy and Leadbelly, recorded versions of the song, and so have contemporary rock and pop groups. *See See Rider* has also been called *C.C. Rider* and *Easy Rider.*

My arrangement of *See See Rider,* based upon several guitar versions of the piece, uses a repeating left hand pattern to support the melody in the right hand. First practice each hand separately, paying special attention to the steadiness of the left hand.

See See Rider's left hand pattern is called an *alternating* bass because the notes alternate between high and low pitches.

Notice, however, that there is a slight change in measure four: the single repetition of D adds a little more rhythm to the piece, and this is the kind of variation that blues musicians frequently use.

In the sixth measure, and again in measure ten, the right hand melody is played on the offbeat. This, too, is an important technique in blues and will be discussed further on page 13. When you've learned each part separately, put it together and let the alternating bass, flowing back and forth, carry the piece at a moderate tempo.

See See Rider

Traditional
Arranged by Eric Kriss

Playing off the Beat

One important element that characterizes blues music is the syncopated or anticipated beat. Many musicians call this "playing off the beat," meaning that a melody note, or group of notes, is played just before or just after a primary downbeat.

The first three melody notes above fall directly on beats one, two and three, but the fourth note is played between the third and fourth beats. In this case, the fourth beat is *anticipated* in advance; in other words, the fourth melody note sounds before the fourth beat arrives.

This concept of anticipation is vital to the blues because it gives the music a feeling of looseness and swing. Try the exercises below and you'll soon discover that you can develop a driving beat with a "push" anticipation of the right hand.

Cocaine Blues is a classic folk blues that has been recorded many times. This arrangement features a steady alternating bass line (similar to *See See Rider* in the last chapter) with the right hand adding some anticipated, or offbeat, melody notes. Practice the piece slowly at first to learn the correct timing, and then speed it up. *Cocaine Blues* sounds equally good at a fast or moderate pace.

Cocaine Blues

Traditional
Arranged by Eric Kriss

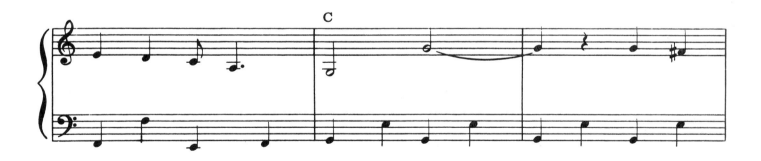

Delta Blues

The blues developed between 1865 and 1900 in the rural American South. One of the most prolific centers of early blues activity was the Mississippi Delta region, extending from Memphis through towns like Natchez and Vicksburg.

Three prominent blues guitarists, Charley Patton, Son House and Robert Johnson, spent time entertaining in the heart of the Delta, notably at Dockery Farms, a plantation established in 1895. Robert Johnson developed a sophisticated blues style that later became the basis of modern Chicago blues. Charley Patton is still remembered in the Delta for his strong vocals, and Son House, who was "rediscovered" in the 1960s, pioneered a plaintive guitar style featuring an alternating bass line.

Dockery Blues, named for this important blues center, captures the essence of the Delta guitar style in a piano arrangement. It has a fourteen-bar chorus, instead of the usual twelve; this was characteristic of early rural blues before the influence of the phonograph "standardized" the blues progression.

The left hand plays a chordal alternating bass instead of the single-note alternating bass used in *See See Rider* and *Cocaine Blues.* The general approach, though, is the same for either single-note or chordal alternating basses.

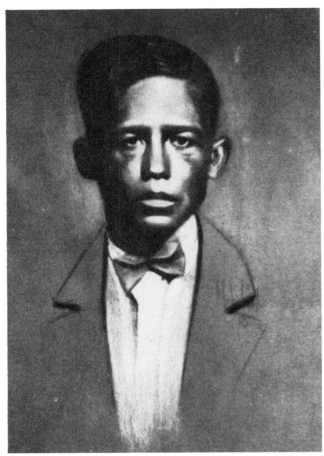

Charley Patton

Play the left hand with a slight "bounce," almost staccato; the overall effect resembles a drone, but by hitting the keys with a light bounce, you will avoid sounding like a steamroller. As in *Cocaine Blues, Dockery Blues* uses offbeats in the right hand (see measures six and eight). Approach the offbeats as you did in *Cocaine Blues* and you won't have any trouble.

Dockery Blues

Eric Kriss

The Flat-Four Beat

Many of the old blues pianists played in run-down shacks called barrelhouses. Often these buildings were literally constructed from beer kegs, and the term barrelhouse was not only an apt description of the shacks, but also a colorful name for the music played inside.

Few, if any, of the early blues pianists could read music; they simply made up their own songs or learned new material by ear as they traveled from barrelhouse to barrelhouse. Not being able to read music was a help in some ways, for these bluesmen never learned the so-called "right" way to use the left hand, nor were they influenced by classical keyboard composers like Bach, Beethoven or Chopin.

The result was the evolution of a new kind of piano playing, totally unlike the classical tradition, that relied upon a repetitious, steady bass line. In notation, the early barrelhouse bass lines look like this:

Musicians call this a *flat-four* beat because each note falls squarely, or flatly, on the beat, and no beat is given more emphasis than another. Here a few barrelhouse flat-four patterns; practice them until there is no unsteadiness or wavering. Although it looks simple, one of the most difficult things in blues piano is to perform the basic bass line without errors. This is the only way you can develop a confident and authentic blues style.

Hayfever Blues is arranged in the early barrel-house style. Note the two-measure introduction, which leads directly into the barrelhouse flat-four bass line. In measure nine, a grace note, or slide, is used; I will discuss this technique further on page 36. Watch the offbeat anticipations carefully, and you will turn *Hayfever Blues* into an exciting, foot-stomping barrelhouse number.

Hayfever Blues

Eric Kriss

Using Triplets

Barrelhouse piano derives much of its charm from the subtle ways in which the right and left hands interact on the keyboard. For instance, the right hand frequently plays offbeat melodies over the steady flat-four bass in the left hand.

Nearsighted Blues, a barrelhouse number like *Hayfever Blues,* uses triplets in the right hand in addition to offbeat melodies. Blues triplets are usually played with the emphasis on the downbeat, as in this sequence:

In *Nearsighted Blues,* the right hand shifts from triplets to dotted eighth-notes, enhancing the rhythmic contrast in the piece. These exercises will develop your rhythmic skills so you can master the blues triplets in *Nearsighted Blues.*

Note that a tied triplet is nearly equivalent in rhythm to a dotted eighth-note.

This means that the interchanging triplets and dotted eighths complement, and even anticipate each other rhythmically, and this is part of the secret to the blues feeling in *Nearsighted Blues.*

Nearsighted Blues

Eric Kriss

Boogie Woogie Style

Boogie woogie piano developed in the 1920s and has been popular ever since. The early pioneers—Meade Lux Lewis, Albert Ammons, Jimmy Yancey, Pete Johnson, Cripple Clarence Lofton, and others—created the distinctive boogie bass between 1925 and 1940, and it has changed little over the years.

The boogie woogie bass is syncopated, usually very repetitious, and it outlines the basic blues chord progression. While the left hand carries the rhythm and chord pattern, the right hand "colors" the piece with blues notes and solo lines. Here are a few illustrations of popular boogie woogie bass lines:

Sweet Life Boogie Woogie, an easy-going Texas-style blues, uses a simple chordal boogie woogie bass (see illustration A above). It is extremely important to play the bass line evenly, without pauses or pounding. There is nothing worse than a boogie woogie pianist with a heavy touch—everything ends up sounding like the take-off of a jet airliner. So, with this in mind, practice the bass line to *Sweet Life Boogie Woogie* lightly, and without the pedal, as this tends to slur too many notes together.

The melody to *Sweet Life* is fairly simple, although a few of the notes are played on the offbeat. The difficult part is putting the two hands together. As a learning aid, I suggest breaking down the boogie woogie bass into a barrelhouse type until you have the skill to play both hands together.

Then you can move back into boogie woogie style, and play the piece as it's written.

Perform *Sweet Life* at a moderate tempo, without rushing. You may wish to use a metronome at first, until you're familiar with the boogie woogie syncopated rhythm.

Sweet Life Boogie Woogie

Eric Kriss

Jimmy Yancey Style

While most boogie woogie pieces feature bass lines similar to *Sweet Life Boogie Woogie* in the last chapter (i.e., syncopated chordal type), Jimmy Yancey and other Chicago pianists introduced a single-note boogie woogie bass in the 1930's.

Single-note boogie woogie basses, as opposed to the flat-four barrelhouse single-note basses, are syncopated and thus have notes played on the off-beat. *South Side Shuffle,* named for the South Side of Chicago where Jimmy Yancey lived, and modeled after his style, uses a syncopated bass with an almost Latin flavor:

Notice that the first and third notes fall on the beat, while the middle note in the pattern falls on the offbeat. This technique gives the bass a kind of "push," allowing the right hand to take a more secondary position. To help you get the feel of the syncopation, first try counting: 1 2 3/1 2 3/1 2 3 rapidly several times. On each count of **1** clap your hands (make sure to count the numbers out loud). Then try adding a foot tap on every other number, starting with the first **1**. The pattern looks like this:

1 2 **3**/**1** 2 **3**/**1** 2
 *   *   *

The numbers in bold face indicate foot taps, and the * represents a handclap. If you begin slowly, at about two counts per second, you should be able to work up the pattern to a respectable tempo in about forty-five minutes of concentrated effort. After that, the rest is simple (relatively speaking, that is).

Read through the right hand melody until you understand the general timing involved, and then put the two hands together. You'll notice that *South Side Shuffle* has a complicated rhythmic interplay when both hands perform together, in spite of the fact that the hands played separately appear almost simple-minded. Taking simple patterns and combining them in a complex manner is one of the most difficult musical skills and one of the assets of a good blues pianist.

Jimmy Yancey, Mrs. Yancey, Clarence Lofton

South Side Shuffle

Eric Kriss

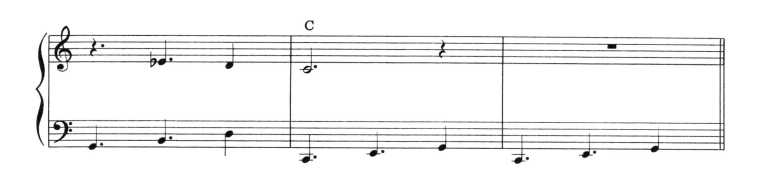

The Walking Bass

Blues pianists have always adopted elements of other styles of music, especially jazz, which has enjoyed a separate, yet parallel, evolution to the blues. In the 1930s, economic conditions often forced clubs and concert halls to hire fewer musicians and, not surprisingly, the piano player became immensely popular because he could play unaccompanied.

To "supplement" their unaccompanied acts, many pianists made an effort to sound like a larger group; one of the most successful techniques was to "borrow" the jazz lines that bassists played in big bands. This style of playing, known as a *walking bass,* was quickly incorporated into the blues tradition.

Walk 'Em On Down Blues, inspired by bluesman Roosevelt Sykes and blues-based organist Jimmy Smith, illustrates the walking bass. Observe that the right hand chords are fuller and more complex than those in earlier lessons, but that the right hand is mostly backing up the left; the reverse was true in the other compositions.

Walk 'Em On Down Blues will also give you a chance to acquaint yourself with some of the lower notes on the keyboard. All too often, piano players forget the wide range of the piano and the rich textures and voicings that are possible on the instrument.

When you practice the bass line, be aware of the chord changes and where the progression is heading. "Listening" like this is the best way to avoid getting lost in the middle of the chorus, which is an easy thing to do if you only concentrate on what bass note comes next.

Roosevelt Sykes

Walk 'Em On Down Blues

Eric Kriss

The Barrelhouse Stomp

Back in the days of the country barrelhouse, one of the most requested piano styles was the *stomp*, a rough, foot-banging version of the blues. Unlike the straight barrelhouse flat-four or boogie woogie, stomps generally have simple bass lines that hit the important downbeats right on the nose. Very little is left to the imagination.

Nagging Woman Blues, arranged in the eight-bar form, is a hard-hitting stomper that, when played correctly, will get everyone out of their seats. The key to the piece is the coordination, or better, the cooperation, between the two hands.

The left hand sets up the basic outline of the chords and emphasizes the downbeats (beats one and three), while the right hand balances with a sharp melody thrown in on the second beat. The overall effect produces the illusion that the melody begins on an off beat, and this, in turn, underscores the importance of the third beat.

Although *Nagging Woman Blues* is a real foot-banger, that doesn't give your hands a license to become feet themselves on the keyboard. Pounding is never a becoming technique, even when used in the roughest blues. The idea is to obtain a heavy, swinging beat without actually smashing the piano with your fingers.

Nagging Woman Blues

Eric Kriss

Using Slides

In the first two lessons, I discussed blues notes, special tones which are located "in-between" the keys of the piano and give the blues its distinctive tonality. In playing blues melodies, pianists use slides, or grace notes, to give their music the right blues "color" (this technique was introduced briefly on page 20).

The blues slide on the piano is performed with *one* finger if the movement is from a black to a white key, or *two* fingers if the slide is from a white to black, or white to white key. Let's examine the one-finger slide first:

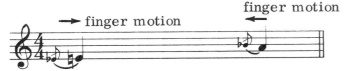

The slide is notated as a grace note and should be performed in a single motion of the finger; in other words, the finger literally slips off one key onto another. Practice the slides notated below until your finger motion glides evenly and the sound is controlled.

The two-finger slide is a little more involved, requiring a slight twist of the wrist as the fingers hit the keyboard. At first, try hitting both keys in the slide simultaneously with a straight wrist. Then turn your wrist as you hit the keys until the notes are separated, producing the slide effect. Here are a few examples to try:

Occasionally, a blues slide will include several notes (white and black keys) which requires the use of more than two fingers. The technique here is the same as in the two-finger slide.

Professor Longhair

Goin' To Gilroy is a slow, gospel-inspired blues that incorporates many of the techniques discussed in this book. A rich blues tonality is obtained by voicing the left hand in full octaves, and the chord substitutions in the right hand add harmonic tension, the counterpart to rhythmic anticipation.

When you've memorized the written arrangement, try adding a few variations of your own invention (you might borrow phrases from other blues in this book to begin with). You now have enough basic ''tools'' to improvize on your own, and improvization is the pathway to further development as a blues pianist.

Goin' To Gilroy

Eric Kriss

Early Rhythm & Blues

Rhythm and blues, the forerunner of rock and roll, evolved in response to the development of electric amplification. The electric guitar was a novelty in the 1940s, but gained steadily in popularity. As the volume increased, bands became more raucous and rhythmic.

The piano player, however, had a rough time adapting to the new electric sound (the first electric pianos, though commonplace today, didn't appear until many years later). To make up for this lack of amplification, pianists developed a repetitious, pounding style that at least allowed them to be heard above the din of the band.

Jukebox Jane, a title commemorating all those 1950s teenage girls who whiled away afternoons at soda shops, is written in the style of many early rhythm and blues tunes. The chord progression departs from the typical 12-bar blues pattern, but the feel is still very much rooted in the blues.

Play the right-hand triplets evenly, without hesitation, and make sure the piece has a constant push to it. If you know a drummer and bass player, you should be able to mimic the r&b sound; have the drummer play triplets on the hi-hat and half notes with his kick, while the bass plays the same line as the piano.

"Tuts" Washington

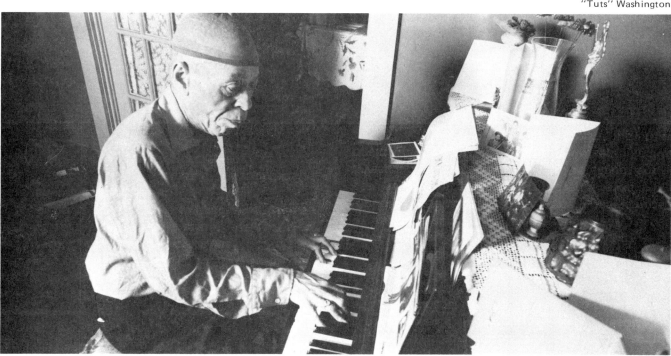

Jukebox Jane

Eric Kriss

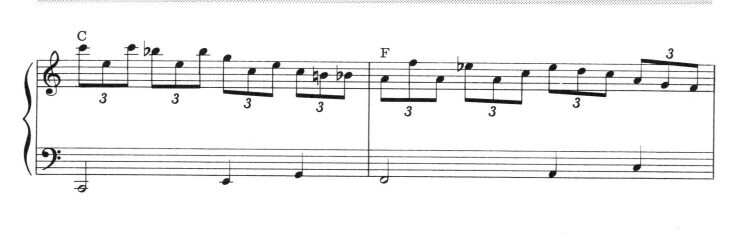

The Gospel Feel

Gospel music has always had a strong influence on the blues. In fact, many musicians claim gospel and blues are the same music—just substitute "God" for "baby" in the lyrics, they say, and you can change a blues into a gospel tune.

It's not really that easy. Gospel music is richly harmonic and uses distinctive rhythmic patterns. For example, *The Gospel Keys* is in 3/4 time and if you had a few friends clapping along, their timing would be: rest, clap, clap/rest, clap, clap/ and so on.

The chord structure in *The Gospel Keys* doesn't follow a blues progression; chord inversions give the piece a unique harmonic quality. Look at the sixth measure. The right hand plays a G major triad, but the left plays a D octave in the bass (this is called the "second" inversion of G). Then in the next measure, the right hand plays a C major triad, but the left plays an E octave in the bass (this is called the "first" inversion). These inversions give the piece a soulful gospel flavor.

The ending is a "fade out," meaning you play as long as you wish, as you gradually lower the volume as much as possible without slowing down. On records you can hear this type of ending frequently; if you tape record yourself at home, try getting the same effect by having a friend work the volume control.

Ray Charles

The Gospel Keys

Eric Kriss

repeat 'till fade

Pattern Basses

Pattern basses—bass lines that follow a complex repetitive melody—are the basis of many modern funk and soul songs. The so-called "motown" sound, for example, was largely supported by a pattern bass line like this:

Funk and soul are both outgrowths of blues and share the same approach to chord progressions and blues notes. Many funk tunes use the three standard blues chords and a 12-bar form.

Practice the pattern bass alone at first. Repetition is the key; after playing the same riff hundreds of times, it just becomes second nature. When the pattern is solid and you know it by heart, then add the right-hand "sweetening."

If you have access to other keyboards (like an electric piano, synthesizer, or organ), you can create a great variety of sound textures using this pattern as a foundation. Knowing a few pattern basses is also useful for jam sessions because it gives everyone some common ground to work from. As a piano player, you'll find much of the responsibility for providing a solid pattern will fall on your shoulders (or fingers).

Lucky Funk

1st time left hand only
2nd time both hands

Eric Kriss

Moderately
C6

F

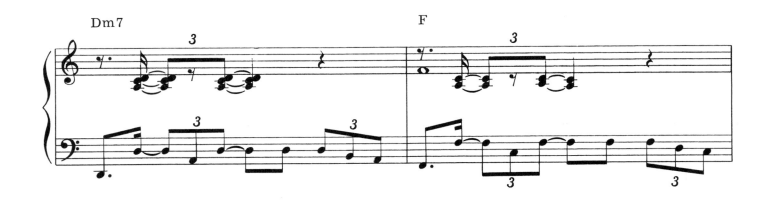

Disco Dynamo

Eric Kriss

Funk Crusade

Eric Kriss

Modern Boogie

When you've progressed this far, you're certainly ready for more challenges. *Bop Bop Boogie* is a more complex blues that uses fast right-hand riffs over a single-note bass line. Play the piece slowly at first, and then work up speed. Once you've mastered this one, check out the other books and records listed in the back; they'll provide ideas and techniques for new directions.

Bop Bop Boogie

Eric Kriss

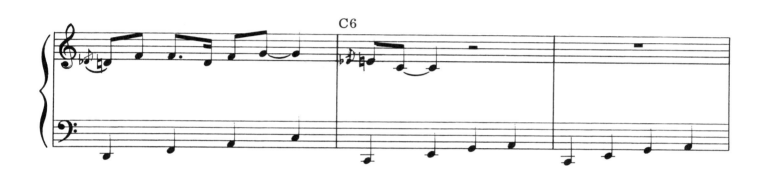

Learning to Improvise

In all the years I have spent playing, teaching, and writing about music, the question I have been asked most often by aspiring blues musicians is: "How can I learn to improvize?"

I'm always ready with my three-word reply: "You already can!" I'm now going to spend some time explaining what "improvising" is all about, how it applies to the blues, and how to use the skills you *already* possess to expand your musical expressions.

Every day, in the normal course of our lives, we are improvising; in fact, the very complexity of our human brains makes it impossible not to do so. We aren't pre-programmed machines that do the same things over and over again. In order to better explain my concept of improvization, I'd like to make the analogy to spoken conversation.

Suppose you're walking down the street and you see a friend who says, "Hey, how are you doin'?" Now it's your turn to take a solo. Thousands of thoughts and impressions flash through your mind in a matter of microseconds. You might say you're okay, terrible, or getting by. You might ask your friend a question, mention something you have in common, or just treat his question as a matter-of-fact greeting, wave to him, and keep walking.

In this situation, you are searching for the *idea* behind your eventual response. Let's suppose you decide to say you're okay. With the idea in mind, you start to *improvise* the actual sentence. "I'm fine, just fine, man," you blurt out. That's the first part of your solo, and in blues it's called a "riff."

Next, you might expand on that first riff by embellishing your answer: "Yeah, I'm fine because I just bought this great book called *How To Play Blues Piano.*" Well, that's the end of the first chorus. If you continue talking in the same vein, that's like taking a couple of choruses; each time you're giving more information as you build upon a central idea (in this case, the fact that you're fine).

Suppose your friend changes the subject completely by mentioning his 1957 Chevy that he just

Victoria Spivey

bought for $8 at a local junkyard. In blues, that would be a key or tempo change. You start to make adjustments in your own conversation; you delete some items, add others, speak more authoritatively (if you know about cars), or more passively (if they bore you to death). That's what improvization is all about. It's the process of expressing your own feelings and ideas, and every day of your life you're actively involved in this process.

You already know how to talk, of course, so this analogy might appear a little silly; after all, you're reading this book to learn about blues piano. The process of learning a language and learning to improvize music is nearly identical. With only a few words and a handful of sentence structures, you can't say much that's original. But as your vocabulary improves, as you learn more set expressions (riffs again), and as you listen to others talk, your own conversation becomes more and more unique.

Now let's see how this process relates directly to blues piano. The first concept is the *idea* (remember: you decide to say you're okay). Is your solo going to be sorrowful, happy, sombre, light-hearted, serene? At first, it might help to actually sketch out on a piece of paper what your idea is. I write musical ideas by using a special kind of "ear graph" like this:

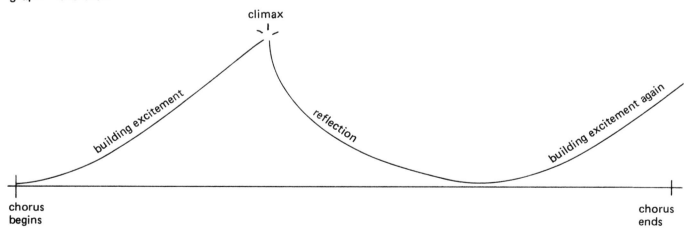

"Ear graph" for a one-chorus solo

This gives me an outline of a musical idea that I can then translate into riffs and embellishments. You might also try sketching on music paper (one stave will usually be sufficient) and let the height of the line represent notes. Here is an example:

A line graph on a stave like this

might translate into a musical phrase like this

When the idea is firmly in your head, or on paper, then it's time to find your first riff. If you've learned all the pieces in this book, you already have lots of material to work with. You can "cut out" phrases from several pieces, mix them up, blend them together until you've created a riff. (In the beginning, you can just steal one from someone else; as the saying goes, if you steal ideas from one person, it's called plagiarism, but if you steal from several, it's called research.)

I'm going to begin simply by stealing this riff from *South Side Shuffle*:

My first task, just as in conversation, is to add more information, to embellish what I've already played. Here are a few examples of variations I might use:

On the extra staves below, try writing in a few of your own variations.

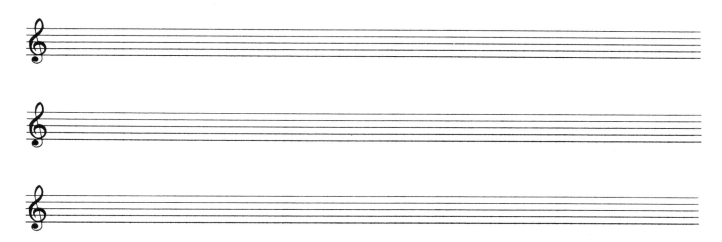

Inventing interesting new variations is an endless task, and it's not unusual for me to spend *days* working out some new idea. Don't be discouraged if, within the first two minutes, you can't come up with any brilliant ideas. This just takes time and there are no shortcuts.

The next step is putting all the variations together to express the general idea you have in mind. This is one example of a complete chorus (12 bars):

The final piece in this book, aptly named *Graduation Groove*, combines many blues piano techniques within a framework to help you test out your improvising skills. At the beginning, all the notes and riffs are written out (the tune has one theme and a solo middle section), but on the third repeat of the theme (see the 24th bar) you'll notice that the right-hand stave is blank!

Now you're on your own. Play the written riffs over and over, and then venture out, testing your musical ideas with your ear. Starting with the 31st bar, the spotlight is on you for an 8-bar *improvised* solo. Use *Graduation Groove* as a springboard for developing your natural talent with all that you've learned.

The important thing to remember is that you already know about the *process* of improvising. You now must take that process and apply it to the piano. Good luck!

Graduation Groove

Easy, with swing

Eric Kriss

To Coda
(2nd time)

fill in riff here

fill in riff here

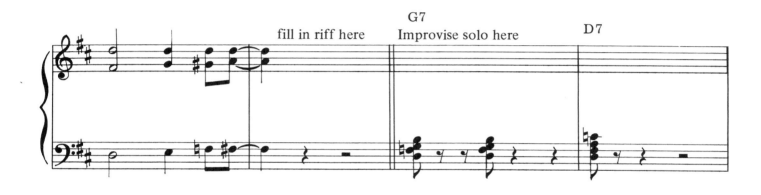

G7

fill in riff here

Improvise solo here

D7

G7

D7

G7

D7

D.C. al Coda

Coda

rit.

trem.

Other Piano Books

If you enjoyed *How To Play Blues Piano,* and wish to continue your exploration of blues piano, I have written two other books on an intermediate/advanced level to assist your studies.

Six Blues-Roots Pianists (Oak Publications, $3.95) is an in-depth study of six influential bluesmen—Jimmy Yancey, Roosevelt Sykes, Champion Jack Dupree, Speckled Red, Otis Spann and Little Brother Montgomery. The book contains accurate, note-for-note transcriptions taken directly from old 78 rpm recordings, as well as historical commentary and performance hints.

Barrelhouse and Boogie Piano (Oak Publications, $5.95) is a more general survey of the blues world featuring twenty-two piano bluesmen from a variety of stylistic perspectives. Aside from note-for-note transcriptions, the book contains a recording of original blues solos, exercises, an appendix of important blues bass lines, a discography, and a description of the social and economic forces which shaped blues piano music during the last fifty years.

Selected Discography

Here are ten piano blues records to begin your collection (if you haven't begun one already). I've included the addresses of the record companies since these LPs are often difficult to locate; if you can't find them at your local speciality record store, write to the company directly and ask for a catalog and price list.

Archive of Folk Music (10920 Wilshire Boulevard, West Los Angeles, CA 90024)
FS 216 Otis Spann
FS 217 Champion Jack Dupree

Arhoolie Records (Box 9195, Berkeley, CA 94709)
F 1076 Dave Alexander: The Rattler

Delmark Records (4243 North Lincoln, Chicago, IL 60618)
601 Speckled Red: The Dirty Dozens
626 Piano Blues Orgy: Sunnyland Slim, Little Brother Montgomery, Otis Spann, Roosevelt Sykes and others

Inner City Records (43 West 61 Street, New York, NY 10023)
IC 1010 Roosevelt Sykes
IC 1011 Memphis Slim

Music Minus One (43 West 61 Street, New York, NY 10023)
MMO 4089 Eric Kriss: Blues Fusion (instructional play-along album)
MMO 1011 Mal Waldron: The Blues Minus You (instructional album)

Yazoo Records (54 King Street, New York, NY 10014)
L 1028 Barrelhouse Piano: Cow Cow Davenport, Barrelhouse Welch and others

About the Author

Eric Kriss is a pianist, record producer, and writer with extensive experience in the field of music education. He recently produced Michael Bloomfield's album for *Guitar Player,* and his own album, *Blues Fusion,* was released in 1976 by Music Minus One. Mr. Kriss has written three books on the art of blues piano playing, and is a frequent contributor to *Downbeat, Living Blues, Contemporary Keyboard,* and other music periodicals. In addition to his own performing career, he has helped issue records by veteran bluesmen like Roosevelt Sykes and Memphis Slim.